Seriously, CINDERELLA IS SO ANNOYING!

The Story of
CINDERELLA
as Told by THE WICKED STEPMOTHER

by Trisha Speed Shaskan   illustrated by Gerald Guerlais

PICTURE WINDOW BOOKS
a capstone imprint

Special thanks to our adviser, Terry Flaherty, PhD, Professor of English,
Minnesota State University, Mankato, for his expertise.

⁓⁓☙❧⁓⁓

Editor: Jill Kalz
Designer: Lori Bye
Art Director: Nathan Gassman
Production Specialist: Sarah Bennett
The illustrations in this book were created digitally.

⁓⁓☙❧⁓⁓

Picture Window Books
1710 Roe Crest Drive
North Mankato, MN 56003
www.capstonepub.com

⁓⁓☙❧⁓⁓

Library of Congress Cataloging-in-Publication Data
Shaskan, Trisha Speed, 1973–
Seriously, Cinderella is SO annoying! : the story of Cinderella as
told by the wicked stepmother / written by Trisha Speed Shaskan ;
illustrated by Gerald Guerlais.
p. cm. — (The other side of the story)
Summary: The classic tale of Cinderella is told by her stepmother, who
was not really so wicked after all.
ISBN 978-1-4048-6674-4 (library binding)
ISBN 978-1-4048-7048-2 (paperback)
[1. Fairy tales. 2. Humorous stories.] I. Guerlais, Gerald, ill. II. Title.
PZ8.S3408Se 2012
[E]—dc22   2011006994

Printed in the United States of America in Stevens Point, Wisconsin.
052013   007437R

You must have heard of me. The *wicked* stepmother? Not true. It's just another one of Cinderella's wild stories. Not as wild as the one about the pumpkin. And the fairy godmother. The *real* story, the *true* story, began with some chatter—and some dust.

3

All I ever wanted was a husband and a mansion. Before I married Cindy's father, my two darlings and I had met Cindy only a few times. The girl had *seemed* normal then.

After I married Cindy's father, my darlings and I moved in. When I had just one foot on the front step, my dear husband kissed me good-bye and said, "I'm off on business!"

"He leaves often," Cindy said, "but the animals stay put. They talk. They joke. They sing. They even help out—especially the bluebirds."

4

Now, I don't mind a story. But I like facts, not fiction. Soon the girl was talking all kinds of hokey-pokey.

"Once upon a time," Cindy said, "one of the bluebirds became blue. Not the color. The feeling. His friend had flown south …"

My darlings and I were stuck near the front door. I just wanted to put away my bags. And that's when I saw it: dust.

"Dear, is the whole house this dusty?" I asked.

"I don't know," Cindy said. "I'll give you a tour!"

In the dining room,
Cindy told stories.

In the study, Cindy told stories.

Nonstop.

"Girls," I said, "time to get to work. This place needs a good cleaning."

"Once upon a time, when I was cleaning ..." Cindy started.

Oh, boy.

Cindy mopped the floor. But she finished so fast!
My darlings had barely started.

"Did you know robins and sparrows are my
friends?" she said. "But the sparrows don't like
the robins. Silly creatures! Once upon a time, one
of the robins—"

"Cindy, dear," I said, "why don't you go and wash
the clothes now, hmm?"

But Cindy washed them so fast! How on earth did she do it? I had to find another chore for her, just to keep her busy.

"If there's one thing squirrels love, it's washing clothes," Cindy said. "The rats, though, would rather iron. You know, one day I—"

"Squirrels and rats doing laundry? Quit telling such foolish stories!" I said.

Time passed, but nothing changed.

In the garden, Cindy
told stories.

In the kitchen, Cindy told stories.

At dinner, I couldn't hear myself think.
"Dear, please," I said,

"STOP TALKING!"

But Cindy didn't stop.

One day, a letter arrived. It was an invitation to the king's ball. The prince would surely fall in love with one of my darlings. Then they would marry, live in a beautiful castle, and one day be king and queen of all the land!

"Oh, Stepmother, I have to go too!" said Cindy. "Once upon a time, a girl and a prince …"

And then—just like that—Cindy lost her voice. Imagine! It had to be from all that storytelling.

Well, what could I do? I told Cindy she had to stay home—for her health. She cried, of course. But a ball was no place for a sick girl. She needed rest.

Sometimes, it's so hard being a stepmother.

At the ball, my darlings twirled. They whirled.

But then some strange girl waltzed in.
Her gown was magnificent. I couldn't take
my eyes off it. I wondered how much it cost
and if my seamstress could copy it for me.

The prince and the girl danced and pranced.
My poor darlings were left prince-less.

A few days later, the prince made an announcement. A glass slipper had been left at the castle. The prince would marry the girl whose foot it fit. Our big chance!

After visiting every other mansion in the neighborhood, the prince's valet arrived at our door.

"Me! Me!" said one of my darlings.

"No, me! Me!" said the other.

"One at a time," said the valet.

Each girl tried, but the shoe didn't fit.

Then Cindy pushed out a whisper.
"Please—let—me—try."

The shoe fit! Cindy pulled the match out of her pocket.

"Whaaaaaaat?" my darlings cried.

Cindy pushed out another whisper. She said something about a "pumpkin coach" and "mice that turned into horses." She even added a "fairy godmother." Please! There's no such thing!

But I still don't know where she got those shoes ...

A few days later, the prince married Cindy. Poor man. He had no idea what he was getting himself into. But *we* lived happily ever after!

22

Think About It

Read a classic version of *Cinderella*. Now look at the stepmother's version of the story. List some things that happened in the classic version that didn't happen in the stepmother's version. Then list some things that happened in the stepmother's version that didn't happen in the classic. How are the two stories different?

Most versions of *Cinderella* tend to be told from an invisible narrator's point of view. But this version is from the stepmother's point of view. Which point of view do you think is more honest? Why?

If you could be one of the main characters in this version of *Cinderella*, who would you be, and why? The stepmother or one of the stepsisters? Cinderella? The prince?

How would other fairy tales change if they were told from another point of view? For example, how would *Hansel and Gretel* change if the witch told it? What if the baby bear in *Goldilocks and the Three Bears* told that story? Write your own version of a classic fairy tale from a new point of view.

❧

Glossary

character—a person, animal, or creature in a story

narrator—a person who tells a story

point of view—a way of looking at something

version—an account of something from a certain point of view

Read More

Bradman, Tony. *Cinderella and the Mean Queen*. After Happily Ever After. Mankato, Minn.: Stone Arch Books, 2009.

Jolley, Dan. *Pigling: A Cinderella Story: A Korean Tale*. Graphic Myths and Legends. Minneapolis: Graphic Universe, 2009.

McClintock, Barbara. *Cinderella*. New York: Scholastic Press, 2005.

Internet Sites

FactHound offers a safe, fun way to find Internet sites related to this book. All of the sites on FactHound have been researched by our staff.

Here's all you do:

Visit www.facthound.com

Type in this code: 9781404866744

Look for all the books in the series:

Believe Me, Goldilocks Rocks!
Honestly, Red Riding Hood Was Rotten!
Seriously, Cinderella Is SO Annoying!
Trust Me, Jack's Beanstalk Stinks!

Super-cool stuff!

Check out projects, games and lots more at
www.capstonekids.com